IMAGES OF ENGLAND

NUNEATON
VOLUME II

CHILVERS COTON CH. (SHEPPERTON) 326.

IMAGES OF ENGLAND

NUNEATON
VOLUME II

PETER LEE

TEMPUS

Frontispiece: Chilvers Coton Church, Shepperton.

First published 2004

Tempus Publishing Limited
The Mill, Brimscombe Port,
Stroud, Gloucestershire, GL5 2QG
www.tempus-publishing.com

British Library Cataloguing in Publication Data.
A catalogue record for this book is available from the British Library.

ISBN 0 7524 3242 7

Typesetting and origination by Tempus Publishing Limited.
Printed and bound in Great Britain.

Contents

Happy girls taking part in the Nuneaton Hospital carnival of 1931.

Introduction

I am most grateful to Tempus Publishers for asking me to produce a sequel to my original book of old photographs and reminiscences covering the Warwickshire town of Nuneaton. The town is in the very centre of England. The first book sold out and has had to be reprinted. With this volume, I intend to concentrate on the way the townscape has changed, and to look at scenes from the lives of several groups of townspeople and individuals, most of whom are no longer with us. You will notice I have not dealt with industry to any extent. It is hoped that I can concentrate on that in future book(s), particularly railways and heavy industry. Here I have confined my industrial scope mainly to lighter industries – wool, cotton, textiles, clothing and engineering. These trades took over from the silk trade, the staple industry of the town in the first half of the nineteenth century. The demise of the silk trade in the late 1850s led to great distress but it took another twenty years for cloth and clothing manufacturers to provide work for those hands who had so heavily relied on the manufacture of fine silks.

In 2003 I lost more of those old friends who have helped in my research: Maurice Billington, a wonderful old Nuneaton character, and fellow railway buff, David Stubbs. I would also like to remember and thank the late Fred Phillips, Arthur Tooby, Mick Lee, Peter Bayly, Phillip Vernon, Reg Rowley, Harold Lapworth, Bill Holloway, Charles Mallabone, all of whom passed on a wealth of information in times past, but are no longer able to contribute their great knowledge to the story of the town and its community.

Thankfully I still can rely on Alan Cook, Vic Holloway, Jean Lapworth, Beryl Kerby, Moreton Ensor in the U.S.A., Anne Paling Lawson, R.P. Neath, and John Webber for their invaluable help.

A lot of this photographic material came from my late friend, Geoff Edmands and his brother Ronald. Geoff would go out on photographic missions with his cousin Reg Bull and record the local scene particularly in the 1950s, '60s and '70s. They were so enthusiastic about recording scenes of everyday life which have become 'Images of the Past'. Thanks also to Madge Edmands who has helped in the creation of this record.

I hope I have remembered everyone in captioning these photographs. Many of the photographs came to me third- and fourth-hand from postcard sales and from unnamed sources so I have marked these 'Author's Collection'.

I would also like to thank Bea Phillips, Steve Moore, John Burton, Steve Casey, Keith Draper and many more for their help. To our local newspapers: the *Coventry Evening Telegraph* and the *Heartland Evening News*. In addition, the resources of Warwickshire County Council, Records Office and Libraries Service.

If you are interested in our local Nuneaton Heritage there are dedicated websites for you:

Local History, www.nuneaton-online.org.uk
Family History, www.nnwfhs.org.uk

Peter Lee, 2004

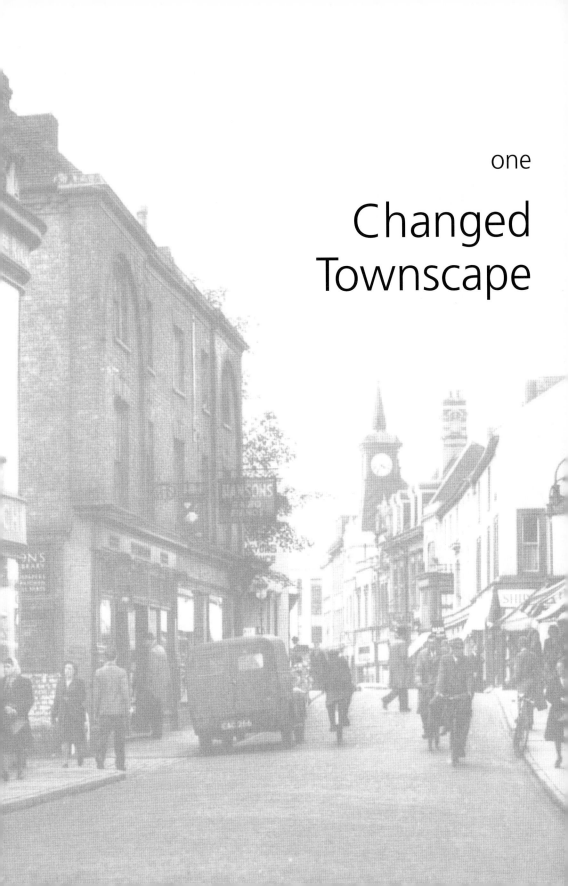

one

Changed
Townscape

MARKET PLACE, NUNEATON 8091

The Market Place in the early 1960s. On the extreme left is the White Swan public house shortly to be closed and demolished, then Marks & Spencer, followed by Turner's shoe emporium, leading to the dominant edifice, which is now Barclays Bank. On the right is W. Cawthorne & Sons, stationers and printers whose business was originally started in the 1830s by Thomas Short, then the National Provincial Bank on the corner of Newdigate Square. The row of shops leading up to the familiar town clock includes Iliffes the Chemist, established during the first half of the nineteenth century. Facing us are Burton's the tailors, and the Maypole grocers. (Author's Collection)

Opposite above: The old Bridge Street looking towards the Market Place gave the approach to the town a quaint claustrophobic appearance. Just behind the van a 'jitty' ran off down to the flourmill. Just imagine how the mill's Sentinel steam wagons negotiated this narrow turn. It would have stopped traffic for a time as it backed out and backed in. On the extreme left you can just see the rear entrance to the Granby's Head pub (formerly the Marquis of Granby), Richmonds Home Furnishers where generations of Nuneaton newly-weds bought their three-piece suites, sideboards and bedroom furniture. Beyond that W.H. Smith, the newsagents and booksellers, and Hansons, piano dealers, purveyors of radio sets, and sheet music can be seen. (Author's Collection)

Opposite below: In 1959, all these fine old buildings were demolished. At the time there was scant interest in old buildings in the town. Large swathes of Nuneaton were unceremoniously torn down without regard to their history or value as treasured parts of our townscape. I can think of the Board Inn in the Market Place, a picturesque eighteenth-century pub; the Kings Head in Church Street which dated back to the sixteenth century and still served the beer from mighty casks stacked at the back of the bar, dispensed direct from the spigot into the glass or jug. Also lost were George Eliot's old school which would be a national treasure had it survived; and timber framed buildings in Abbey Street, packed with history. After this block of buildings was removed it was possible for a time to get an uninterrupted view of the town mill, through the gap on the left. The photograph is dated 1 November 1959. (Geoff Edmands)

BRIDGE STREET, NUNEATON   M 3282

Bridge Street was rebuilt like this. Do you think it is an improvement? Now we see these 1960s buildings as rather plain and uninspiring but at the time they were exciting and gave the town a fresh look of new confidence. The real reason they were built, however, was to allow the car to gain access to the town centre. Now that cars have been almost banned from entering the town, the old buildings could have stayed. Hindsight is a wonderful thing. (Author's Collection)

Looking towards Bridge Street with the mass of the blue brick flourmill behind the photographer, this once-in-a-lifetime exposure gives us a glimpse of a long forgotten townscape.
1 November 1959. (Geoff Edmands)

Looking west towards Coton Road from the top of St Nicolas parish church tower – the dazzlingly new inner ring road has been built. It provided much relief for the volume of traffic in the town. The large building in the background is our beloved Courtaulds Mill. This picture is dated 19 March 1966 (Geoff Edmands)

Opposite above: Redevelopment in the '60s saw the Old Granby Head pub demolished to be replaced by this brick box, now that popular local 'bunny run' venue, Bilberries. The photograph was taken on 22 July 1961. You can see the old Church Street buildings beyond are still intact at this date but they would not last long. (Geoff Edmands)

Opposite below: Other developments followed in quick succession. The old Midland Red bus garage was demolished and a new one built in Newtown Road. Here you can see the last steel supports still standing on 16 July 1960. The buildings beyond are the electricity works and beyond that, the flourmill. Demolition of the bus garage enabled the inner ring road over the River Anker to be built. (Geoff Edmands)

Along Vicarage Street from the church tower you can see the extent by which Vicarage Street was widened. On the left, all new developments have taken place, apart from the Parish Hall on the lower left. Beyond is the new magistrates court (which was replaced in 2004 with a new building). The tall edifice is the police station and beyond that what is now the Job Centre. On the right, Wheat Street leads off and hidden in the trees is Vicarage Street School. Up until this work was carried out, Vicarage Street was a narrow lane with many old cottages. On the left where the magistrates court stands was The Elms where George Eliot (Mary Ann Evans 1819-1880) went to school from 1828-1832. Even in 1960 it was hardly altered from her days at school. On the corner of Wheat Street stood two pubs, The Black Horse, and the Heart in Hand. These were frequented by generations of old railwaymen before and after being on duty. (Geoff Edmands)

Opposite above: From the top of St Nicolas parish church tower the photographer has taken this view of the new library with Powell House (government offices), the Labour Exchange and the Social Security office beyond. (Geoff Edmands)

Opposite below: The Roman Catholics were well represented in Nuneaton with this fine church, which stands in Coton Road. When the new ring road into the centre of town was built, part of the burial ground attached to the church was removed. (Author's Collection)

PARISH CHURCH AND THE OLD GRAMMAR SCHOOL, NUNEATON   M 4434

Modernisation of the town centre altered many different facets of the townscape. The Wesleyan Methodist church, which stood on the corner of Stratford Street and Abbey Street, was demolished during September 1963. The buildings exposed by this demolition in Stratford Street have been demolished and a new pub, The Felix Holt stands on this site. The white-faced building just right of the lamp post was the original Methodist church, built for the local Methodist community before they moved away into different persuasions, notably Wesleyan and Primitive Methodists. Shops have now replaced the Wesleyan church. (Geoff Edmands)

Opposite above: A February 1966 view of St Nicholas parish church with the ring road island in the foreground and the old Grammar School on the left, now the parish offices. It is hard to imagine that before the advent of universal education, just a few dozen elite boys in the town learnt to read and write and were taught grammar and Latin. These went on to become the great and good (or not so good) of the local community and beyond, whereas the vast majority were either illiterate or so badly educated as to be barely literate. (Author's Collection)

Opposite below: A contemporary view of the interior of the church. (Author's Collection)

TELEPHONE No. 124.

Artificial Wreaths and Shades,
Crosses and Wire Guards.
Orders taken for Grave Stones,
Brick Graves, Vaults, etc.

Funerals Conveyed any Distance
by Motor Hearse.

ESTABLISHED OVER 100 YEARS.

£1·00

STRATFORD STREET, NUNEATON,
(NO OTHER ADDRESS,)

Feb. 20th 192 3

Mr Reeve

Dr. to **William Smith & Sons,**

UNDERTAKERS.

HEARSE AND MOURNING COACHES.

Partners: AMY SMITH, ALFRED SMITH.

Hearse & pair of Horses & coach & pair	3	10	0

An invoice from William Smith & Sons, undertakers on Stratford Street, sent on 20 February 1923.

Opposite above: The foundation stone for the Wesleyan church, before it was taken away to make way for shops in 1972. (Geoff Edmands)

Opposite below: A fountain stood next to the council house, close to the bus shelters where people used to catch the bus to Coventry before the bus station was opened. Pictured in full spate on 24 August 1959, it was taken away before the present council house was erected. (Geoff Edmands)

BUILT IN 1872
MEMORIAL STONES LAID BY
J. ROBERTS. ESQ?. & S. JEVONS. ESQ?
REBUILT BY R. STANLEY. ESQ? IN 1891
BEING THE CENTENARY YEAR OF THE DEATH OF
REV. JOHN WESLEY. M.A.

Above: At the top of the Bull Ring and into College Street, large parts of Chilvers Coton were demolished so that the new ring road from the Bedworth bypass could enter town. This view is dated 8 July 1965. On the left, properties adjacent to the Jolly Colliers pub have been demolished whilst on the right, the corner shop and attendant cottages wait their turn for demolition. This will all be replaced by a large traffic island with the yellow 'banana' footbridge over it. Even the lovely old Vauxhall car would be a collector's piece today, but has long been turned into paper clips, or steel billets. Just now demolished are the cottages on the left. Regular travellers to the Coventry car factories would store their bikes there for safe keeping before crowding onto the early morning trains. I have heard it mentioned that if you had a puncture when you left your bike, the proprietor of the cycle store would repair it for you so that it was ready for your journey home in the evening. Chilvers Coton railway station was in the gap between the more modern houses in the middle distance and the corner shop. (Geoff Edmands)

People who lived in Nuneaton at the time can often remember what they were doing one winter's evening in December 1967 when one of Nuneaton's largest fires took place. Part of the old Hall & Phillips hat factory in Meadow Street had been taken over by the Awson Carriage Co. who made car parts. I recall visiting there on business a few months before the fire seeing wooden dashboards for the new Triumph Herald and other cars being stacked in piles everywhere. On the evening of 15 December 1967 the works was engulfed in a terrible fire, which lit the blackened town centre for hours. I am not surprised it was so disastrous because the products made, wooden dashboards, coated in varnish were a terrific combustible. This fire removed another old landmark from the Nuneaton townscape. (Geoff Edmands)

Opposite below: The construction of the inner ring road along Coton Road and a new traffic island under Coton Arches likewise gave rise to extensive demolition. On 4 February 1973, Arthur Street was entirely demolished. When Nuneaton presented its case for a new street tramway system in the late 1890s, Arthur Street was suggested as a site for new car sheds and an electricity-generating plant. The tramway system would have stretched from Chilvers Coton to the town centre, to Attleborough, Camp Hill and Stockingford. Despite ten years of discussion, this street tramway never materialised although a gap in the houses in Arthur Street was made for the new car sheds, and the Cock & Bear road bridge was widened. (Geoff Edmands)

New streets and housing estates sprang up throughout the town. This is Donnithorne Avenue, Hill Top estate, looking east towards the new canal bridge, then just completed, on a bleak 4 January 1959. The Donnithorne Arms Public House was erected just beyond the bridge and opened on 3 July 1958. It was named after a pub mentioned in George Eliot's novel *Adam Bede*, the original of which was the Bromley Arms at Ellastone in Staffordshire, Miss Evans' father's home village. The Donnithorne Arms replaced the Heart in Hand pub in Wheat Street, which closed its door the previous day. The Donnithorne Arms was demolished in 1999. (Geoff Edmands)

Opposite above: This is not an aerial photograph but was bravely taken from the top of the old pit heap of Griff No.4 colliery on 6 April 1968. I say bravely because this pit heap burnt constantly for many years due to spontaneous combustion, which had created internal fires which fed off slack coal inside the spoil. Nevertheless it provided a fine vantage point for photographing the new maternity block at the George Eliot Hospital, new housing estates creeping out across formerly open fields, disused coal pits and brickyards that dotted the back of Heath End Road. (Geoff Edmands Collection)

Opposite below: Although the Mill Gardens off Church Street are still there, there have been several changes, even to this view, with altered pathways and changed flowerbeds. The town hall is still there but the electricity works has largely gone, together with the ramshackle of sheds at the rear of the old mill. This picture was probably taken in around 1961. (Author's Collection)

GEORGE ELIOT GARDENS, NUNEATON

L 9171

Above: It is amazing to consider that this building is not a church but is part of the new foundry complex built by Sterling Metals outside of town at Attleborough, seen here on 1 September 1956.

Opposite below: Before the Scala Cinema was built, this fine Georgian house occupied the site and served as the shop premises of Coopers the ironmongers. (Author's Collection)

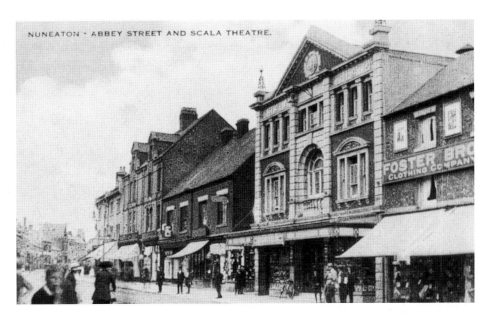

Above: Near the town centre, Abbey Street has outwardly changed less in the last 100 years than any other Nuneaton street. The building on the left of the Scala cinema has been renewed but the others on that side are similar today. The Scala is no longer a cinema. The gap between there and the buildings next door is the 'jitty' leading to Burgage Walk. This walk took you around the back of the poor tenements that festooned Abbey Street over seventy years ago. Court cottages, yards, and 'jitties' were a feature of Nuneaton and all other Midland towns to a greater or lesser extent. Maybe with a degree of vision, some amenity value could have been found in preserving one or two; today little alleyways with shops selling chintzy knick-knacks would be worth exploring for the intrepid shopper and 'jitty' explorer. (Author's Collection)

ABBEY STREET, NUNEATON

L 63

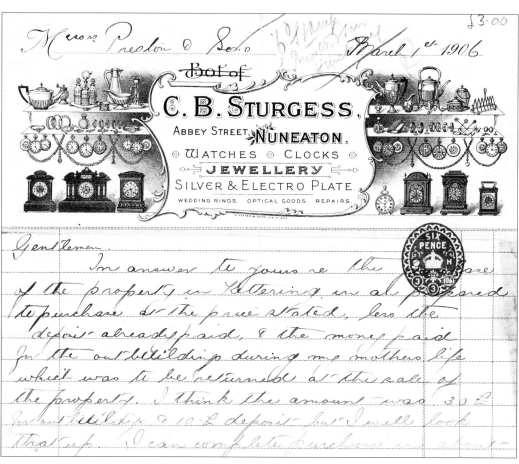

£3·00

Messrs Preston & Son   March 1st 1906

Bot of

C. B. STURGESS,
ABBEY STREET, NUNEATON.
◊ WATCHES ◊ CLOCKS ◊
◄ JEWELLERY ►
SILVER & ELECTRO PLATE.
WEDDING RINGS. OPTICAL GOODS. REPAIRS.

SIX PENCE

Gentlemen.

In answer to yours re the ____
of the property in Kettering in as ____
to purchase at the price stated, less the
deposit already paid, & the money paid
for the outbuilding during my mothers life
which was to be returned at the sale of
the property. I think the amount was 30 £
in outbuilding & 10 £ deposit but I will look
that up. I can complete purchase in about

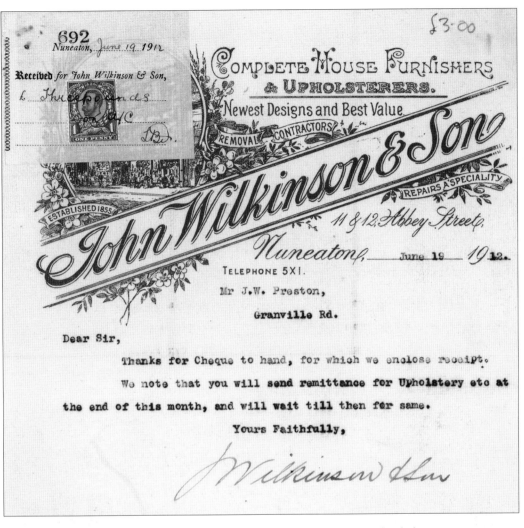

Above: A trade letter from John Wilkinson & Son, house furnishers and upholsterers, sent on 19 June 1912.

Opposite above: A 1950s view of Abbey Street recalls memories of shops now long gone. The shop on the immediate left (no.116) was Wilkinson & Sons. It later became Civic Stores, electrical goods dealers, and is now Staybrite Windows Ltd. Beyond is John Manners Ltd. (formerly The Grand Clothing Hall). Further on is the Children's Shop, then Taylors, Pianos and Television dealers. (Author's Collection)

Opposite below: A letter from C.B. Sturgess, watch, clock and jewellery repairers on Abbey Street, sent on 1 March 1906.

A
GRAND CONCERT

CO-OPERATIVE HALL,
QUEEN'S ROAD, NUNEATON

Sunday, 19th March, 1944, at 7 p.m.

OLIVE GROVES
(SOPRANO)

GEORGE BAKER
(BARITONE)

(London and Provincial Concert and Broadcasting Artistes in Songs & Duets)

WELCOME RETURN OF

The Coventry Hippodrome Broadcasting Orchestra.
Directed by WILLIAM PETHERS

Nuneaton Police and Specials Male Voice Choir.

Conductor: Section/Leader "Reg" Carris.
Accompanist: Section/Leader W. M. Leonard.

DENNIS MILBURN
(Boy Soprano)

ERIC BRIARS
(Violin)

GEORGE WARING
(Singing your Favourites)

ROBERT KEYS
(Pianoforte)

Compere VAN ART, Coventry's Own Comedian

Proceeds in aid of Mayor's Vanquisher Fund and Boys' Hostel.

Programme: Price 3d

An advertisement for a concert by Nuneaton Police and Specials Male Voice Choir, 1944.

Newdegate Arms Hotel

Newdegate Street **Nuneaton** Warwickshire

Telephone Nos. Reception 3656   Visitors 3657, 4777

The present Newdegate Arms replaces a much older house at one time known as the "Black Bull". Recently the public rooms were remodelled and refurnished and the dining room enlarged. The Hotel is in the centre of the busy manufacturing town which has grown around the market square. It is the "Milby" of George Eliot's novels in which the Newdegate Arms figures as the "Oldinport Arms," and is a place of pilgrimage for her admirers. There was a fine Assembly Room in the inn of her day, and the modern Hotel has excellent accommodation for functions. Arbury Hall, seat of the Newdegate family, is open to view on certain days during the summer.

A   T R U S T   H O U S E   H O T E L

1963/64

Above and left: At the very bottom of Newdigate Street stood the Newdigate Hotel. This hotel has been detailed elsewhere in this book but the view of the bottom end of Abbey Street taken in the early 1960s shows a townscape very much changed by later development. The Newdigate is on the left, and the street off to its right but on the left of this view is the extended part of Newdigate Street, or as it was earlier called New Bridge Street. The reason it was called, New Bridge Street was that in 1844 the original bridge, a wooden trestle footbridge, was demolished and a new blue brick bridge replaced it. The new bridge was for both road and pedestrian traffic over the River Anker because horses and carts had, until that time, had to ford the river at this point whilst pedestrians clung to the rickety old wooden trestle bridge. That was not a problem when the Anker was a shallow stream but at times of flood horses have lost their footing and drowned and this gave rise to the improvement at that time. The tall building behind the lamppost was Parsons & Sherwins, the ironmongers, and just beyond there was Parsons and Sherwins' wooden garage. (Geoff Edmand's Collection)

Another view of the bottom of Newdigate Street in the 1980s with Newdigate Square just visible on the left and the Gate Hotel building on the right. Boffin's arcade can be seen to the left in the four-storey modern block. However, this was not known as Newdigate Street in the nineteenth century, but was officially Back Street. The council made a mistake when they renamed the road at the side of the Millennium nightclub Back Street, as that bit of road was originally part of Back Lane. But why was Newdigate Street called Back Street? Because it was the back of the Market Place! Up until the sixteenth century, the Market Place extended back through these buildings to the roadway we see here. This block was not built, but over the years certain market stalls became more permanent, then became shops in their own right and one of these permanent shops is visible in the middle of this photograph. With its traditional pitched roof, it provides the scale of these older buildings in Back Street. In the last twenty years this shop was pulled down and replaced by a modern version on the same scale. It is a pity no one knew about its history; it should have been locally listed as one of the last old shops in Nuneaton town centre. Do you remember Fredericks, where all the young blades around town used to buy their fashionable 'gear' in the '60s and '70s? (Author's Collection)

Opposite above and below: Two Parsons & Sherwin's trade advertisements.

£1·50

Memorandum.

From

EVANS & SONS,

Seedsmen and Florists,

ABBEY STREET,

NUNEATON.

To Messrs Saml Preston & Son

Hinckley.

Dec 27. 188 2

Jny 3

Re John Flint Farmer

Gent: We find the promisory note received from you is short of 5/6 The amt of our a/cts were as follows.

Ironmongery £9 - 17 - 10
Seed { 3 - 2 - 1
12 · 19 · 11

Note received £ 6 - 4 - 6. Kindly explain
the deficiency Yours faithfully
Evans & Sons

Established upwards of 70 years.

EVANS & SONS,

(Late J. H. CLAY),

FURNISHING AND

General Ironmongers,

OIL & COLOR MERCHANTS,

IRON AND STEEL WAREHOUSE,

Agricultural Implement Depot.

Sewing Machines, Washing, Wringing and Mangling Machines, Baths, Trunks, Toilet Ware, &c.

MULLER'S PATENT GAS-MAKING MACHINES

Fitted up in villages or private houses.

Estimates given for fitting up Greenhouses, &c. with Hot=water Apparatus, &c.

Iron Hurdles, Fencing, Wire Netting, Register Grates, Ranges, Marble Chimney Pieces, and all kinds of Builders' Ironwork.

Agricultural & Horticultural Seedsmen.

Agents for the Celebrated Cavendish Bridge Pale Ales and Bitter Beer, and Dublin Stout.

Opposite and above: Evans & Sons. The late J.H. Clay, whose business started in the early 1800s, was a relative of George Eliot (Mary Ann Evans). Samuel Evans (1821-?) had formerly been living on the Arbury Estate where they were estate workers and tenants of the Newdigate Family. They were also related to the Clays through marriage both on the Evans' side, and Mary Ann Evans' mother's side of the family. The shops in the photograph were numbered 128 and 129. Their premises in these lovely old Georgian (or maybe earlier) buildings were almost opposite Abbey Gate. When this advert appeared in the 1870s, the business had only recently been taken over by the Evans family. (Author's Collection)

Moving up Abbey Street just before the First World War, the Gate Hotel, the Liberal Club and the Wesleyan Methodist church are highly visible in this view. On the far right is Nuneaton Co-Operative Society's fine new shop front. Between that and the Wesleyan Methodist church can be seen the original showrooms of Sam Robbins Ltd, the bicycle, and later car dealers. A business started in around 1897 with its headquarters at Rugby and branches at Nuneaton and Willenhall. By 1909, Sam Robbins' motor dealership and repair shop was in Leicester Road in premises that are still associated with the motor trade. It is now a tyre fitters. Next to Sam Robbins is the Weavers Arms public house. This is an appropriate name for a pub in a street which had formally been almost entirely engaged in the silk weaving trade. (Author's Collection)

If you lived in Abbey Street in one of the teeming court cottages, or even in a good front house, you might be faced with this every morning as you crawled out of bed. The plastic bowl is a modern touch as well as the tap. Many people only had a pump in the yard dispensing dirty water. The bottle of California Syrup of Figs on the window ledge kept the owner 'regular'. There are implements for digging the cabbage patch, which passed for a garden outside, and a small shovel probably for removing the cinders from the range. (Author's Collection)

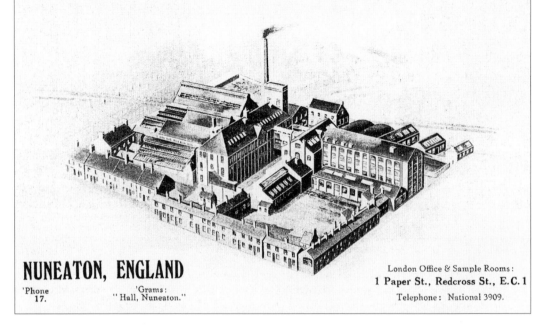

Above: The old established business of Hall & Phillips started in Atherstone in the early 1700s and Joseph Willday purchased the operation in about 1734. The Hall & Phillips proprietorship of the company started in 1853 and in 1890 it was turned into a limited liability company. The original factory on this site was built in 1846 to manufacture silk ribbons (Hood & Ward) but was taken over by Hall and Phillips when they moved to Nuneaton in 1868. Alongside the manufacture of hats was another business, Hall, West & Co. This was an engineering company which made a large range of equipment such as steam boilers, brewing vessels and equipment, pumps, brick making, quarrying and mining equipment. The engineering business was sold in the 1880s to Stanley Brothers, the local brick makers who renamed it the Nuneaton Engineering Company. Stanley's also had an iron foundry at the bottom of Tuttle Hill where castings for use in their patent machinery was made in-house. Hall & Phillips factory was taken over by the Awson Carriage Co Ltd., which made car components.

Overleaf: An aerial photograph taken in October 1965 shows Abbey Green and surrounding streets. The Green is bottom left. The road up to the top left of the picture is Manor Court Road. The road going off to the top right is Midland Road, which joined the bottom of Tuttle Hill just off the picture. The street below it is Aston Road. Where the caravans are parked used to be a group of houses called 'Rose's Patch', after a family named Rose who lived cheek by jowl in a property development that dated from the 1820s for the benefit of their extended family. Abbey Green School can be clearly seen. On the corner of Manor Court Road and Midland Road are two blocks of modern flats built on the site of the former Midland Railway Inn bombed by the Germans in 1942. The large factory (bottom right) is Connor's Box factory, which closed down in 1980. (Geoff Edmands Collection)

Two views of the Baptist Chapel in Manor Court Road in around 1905. Manor Court Road Post Office is the shop on the corner of Botterill Street opposite. It is hard to imagine that twenty to thirty years earlier, this fine wide empty boulevard was a trackway across fields through the old Abbey Site, which was amongst the trees in the distance. (Author's Collection)

The houses on the far right of the Baptist Chapel were bombed during the Second World War.

Abbey Street School, Nuneaton.

Abbey Street School Standard VI and VII young ladies, *c.* 1900–1910. They are all holding their blobby scratchy pens which they frequently dipped into those white pot inkwells. The School Master is Mr T. Daffern. (Author's Collection)

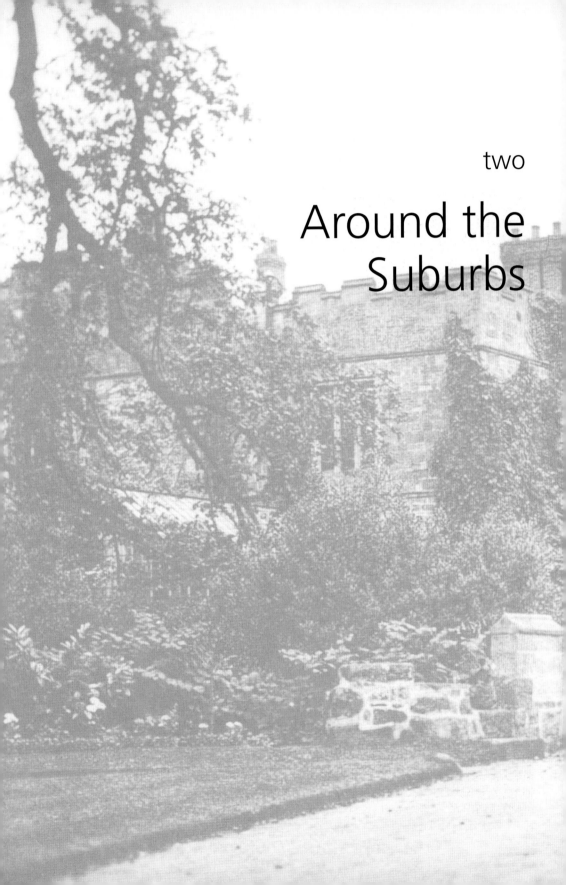

two

Around the
Suburbs

Above: Edward Street was said, at one time, to be one of the longest streets in England, without a pub – if not *the* longest. How true that is I cannot say. Mention was made that it might have been the intervention of leading Methodist townsmen like Reginald Stanley and Joseph Fielding Johnson who influenced not building a pub. It was probably the proximity of other pubs, which militated against it. For example the George and Dragon, the Dugdale Arms, the Rose and the William IV were only a short walk away, so it hardly mattered to the drinking men if they only had a further few yards to stagger. This view is looking towards Queens Road. The white awning of the original single storey Co-op store can just be made out as it stood where High Street now enters Queens Road. It looks as though an old jalopy is doing a three-point turn in the middle of the road. Note too all the cast-iron railings cut down for the war effort. (Author's Collection)

A later view of the Arches after the roadway into Bridge Street on the left had been created through the left hand arch. You are advised to fill up here with Shell at Woods garage who rented space under the right-hand arch. You can glimpse Coton Road under the centre arch as you made your way to Nuneaton town centre. In the arch on the extreme right was a bus garage, Whitehalls, whose buses were one of several operators to take men to the Coventry car factories. Their office was in Henry Street. On the extreme right is Daulman's paper shop. The Daulman family believe their ancestors came from Germany and trace their local ancestry back to a Mr War Daulman who is said to have come over to England from Germany during the early part of the eighteenth century and settled on the Arbury estate, (their ancestry may, however, be more mundane; there was a Wore Dorman in Tamworth in the late seventeenth century). His children were named War and Peace. Quite what the circumstances of his arrival were I do not know, other than to speculate that the Newdigate family must have wished to thank him for deeds on the public behalf and resettled him here in England. There are still Daulman's living at Arbury today. In every generation of their family there has been a son with the Christian name of War! (Author's Collection)

Opposite below: The massive railway bridge we know today as Coton Arches is a familiar and much loved landmark which has stood the test of time. Its wide arch has hardly needed much maintenance considering it has stood for well over 140 years. This is supposedly the second bridge on the site. The first, a tall cast iron structure was probably replaced when there was a series of bridge collapses locally, for example Bedworth in about 1860, Spon End Arches in 1858 and another at Leek Wootton on the branch from Coventry to Leamington Spa at about the same time. The original bridge must have spanned at a great height above a narrow slot where the road went through the embankment. The railway civil engineer decided discretion was the better part of valour and when the 1850 bridge was removed, the embankment was opened out so that these three impressive arches could be inserted. (Author's Collection)

Near to Coton Arches on the corner of Bridge Street going off to the left, and Coton Road to the right, stood the former Nuneaton – Coventry turnpike road toll house. This had gates in both Bridge Street and Coton Road. After the turnpike road was de-turnpiked in the 1870s, the tollhouse was let to a road repaire, and Mr George Adcock and his family lived there for twenty-eight years. In 1913, the toll house was pulled down to widen the road as the building projected out into the roadway. Mr Adcock later went to live in Fitton Street and retired from being Inspector of Roads in June 1936, a time when the local council, rather than the County Council as it is today, was responsible for maintaining the roads. (Dennis Labram collection)

A trade advertisement for J. Whitehall & Son.

Opposite below: This view encapsulates an interesting moment when the Revd M.W. Mansbridge of the Chilvers Coton church set up a small charity stall on the Coton Road near to the Coton Arches, and is engaged in conversation with Dorothy Edmands. A lady waits for the Midland Red bus to take her to the town centre. Woods garage can be seen opposite. (Geoff Edmands)

Above: An aerial view of Avenue Road in October 1965. The New Pingles baths stand out stark in the wide open greenery of the Pingles before it was messed up with running tracks, a pub, and housing. This green lung once stretched right into the town. On the right is the Wem Brook as it snaked its way along the periphery of the Pingles. At one time the houses, which fronted Attleborough Road in the bottom foreground, had long fruitful gardens that stretched open down to the brook. Some still retain this feature. Below the rugger ground you can see a collection from Monty Moreton's bus fleet. On the left of the picture, industrial units are starting to take over the old Caldwell Hall pleasure grounds. Swinnerton School is just off the images on the top right, as is the old school at Coton and what is now the Craft Centre. Off the photograph at the bottom is Attleborough village. (Geoff Edmands Collection)

A rear garden view of old cottages at Chilvers Coton. The zinc bath hangs under the canopy at the rear. (Author's Collection)

Form 3B, Fitton Street School, Chilvers Coton, in about 1926. The only lad I recognise is my father James Walter Lee (1913-1986) who is the boy with the tie seated on the ground, bottom right. (Author's Collection)

Another rear garden view featured the down-pipe with the inevitable peg on the end to redirect the flow of water. Sometimes an old sock replaced this so that the water was slightly cleaner before it drained into the old water butt, which in this case is an old oil drum. (Author's Collection)

Chilvers Coton 'All Saints' parish church, and the old Vicarage before it was demolished. This was essential 'George Eliot Country'; it is much as George Eliot, or Mary Ann Evans (1819–1880), knew it when she lived in the district from 1819-1841. The churchyard is overgrown and nestling under the tree in the foreground is 'Milly's Grave'. (Author's Collection)

A view of the old Chilvers Coton Vicarage, not long before it was demolished in the 1920s. Its structure had become very damp and dilapidated. (Author's Collection)

Chilvers Coton Parish Church.

Inside the old church at Chilvers Coton in tihe 1920s. This was how George Eliot remembered it. (Author's Collection)

Right: In Chilvers Coton churchyard are the graves of George Eliot's family. This one is a monument to her brother, Isaac Pearson Evans (1816-1890). Isaac took over the business that his father had built up in the district, managing the estates of several wealthy landowners, and not just the Newdigates. It involved managing agricultural land, property and valuing the crops in the fields, and timber in the woods etc. When Robert Evans (1773-1849), George Eliot's father retired in 1841, Isaac carried on the business that later passed to his son Walter Pearson Evans. With Isaac in the grave is his wife Sarah Rawlins (1806-1881) and their son, also called Isaac Pearson Evans. (Clare Speight)

Below: Robert Evans' (1773-1849) grave stands in Chilvers Coton churchyard. (Author's Collection)

On the night of 16-17 May 1941, German bombs rained down on Nuneaton. First incendiary bombs lit the night sky to illuminate the target. The enemy bombers were after the railway. Unfortunately for local people that night, they peppered either side of it and incendiaries clattered onto the roof of Coton church. For a time the incendiaries fizzled but did not take hold and could have been knocked off the roof if someone could have reached it with a ladder. Unfortunately it was every man for himself that night, and even if a ladder could have been found it would have been a very brave hero indeed to climb up onto the roof with all that destruction going on as high explosives started blasting the town. This is the result the next morning. The church was destroyed by fire. (Geoff Edmands Collection)

Opposite: Inside the church – a mass of charred beams and rubble. This photograph was taken not long after it was destroyed by German incendiary bombs. (Geoff Edmands Collection)

Left: After the war the church was rebuilt by German Prisoners of War from the nearby Arbury POW Camp. They occupied the huts used by the American Army before D-Day. Most of the Germans held there were classified as low risk 'Wehrmacht' troops who had formerly been tradesmen, teachers and professional people. They were allowed out into the community and were soon befriended by the townsfolk. The vicar of Coton sought recruits amongst them to rebuild the church. Among their number was Karl Weber of Munich, a skilled sculpture whose masterpiece was this statue of Christ on the cross rendered in wire mesh and cement. (Geoff Edmands Collection)

Below: A view taken of the inside of the church after it was rebuilt in 1947. (Geoff Edmands Collection)

Above: The rebuilding has been carried out in a sympathetic style similar to the original but is rather plain. (Geoff Edmands Collection)

Right: An outpost of Chilvers Coton village was at Bermuda. Old cottages on the Arbury estate existed long before Bermuda village was completed in 1891. (Author's Collection)

The gateway to Astley Castle with a bridge over the old moat. (Author's Collection).

Astley Castle was also part of the Arbury Estate in the adjacent hamlet of Astley. It lies at the junction of the main Stockingford to Meriden Road and the road between Bedworth and Ansley. The castle is thirteenth century in origin. (Geoff Edmands Collection)

three

People and
Events

Many of the photographs in this book came from the camera of my old friend Geoff Edmands whose family latterly lived at Coventry Road, Nuneaton. Geoff's cousin Reg Bull, one of Nuneaton's leading amateur photographers and collectors, however, took this photograph. Their adventures together covered a large spectrum of local life. Geoff is pictured here with a pound note, which he has temporarily attached to his radio at 9.44 a.m. on Sunday 10 January 1960 for this photograph. The reason – it has the unique serial number: H43K 1000000. (Geoff Edmands Collection)

Opposite above: The Band of the Junior Leaders Regiment R.A.Corps stationed at Bramcote Barracks halfway between Nuneaton and Wolvey in the Nuneaton Carnival Procession on 18 May 1963, marching along Edward Street. (Geoff Edmands)

Opposite below: Musical Chairs in progress at the Sunday school teacher's social, Chilvers Coton church hall on 7 February 1959. (Geoff Edmands)

Bell ringers in Chilvers Coton church belfry, *c.* 1950. (Geoff Edmands Collection)

Opposite above: Marcus Harry Rouse, a Nuneaton student at the teacher training college at Bristol, repairing Astley church bells in December 1968. When he left King Edward VI Grammar School to attend college as a teacher of handicrafts, he met a girl from Wiltshire who was interested in campanology. This sparked his own interest in bell ringing and led him to research a practical thesis on the subject. As part of his college research he undertook to replace new bell guides, work which kept him at the belfry until early in the morning. (Geoff Edmands Collection)

Opposite below: A local band called the 'The Queens Hall Revels'. The Queens Hall was a popular music venue in Queens Road. This view dates from the late 1920s or '30s. (Anne Lawson Collection)

'THE·QUEENS·HALL·REVELS'

Sarah Townsend (1816-1907) was the daughter of William and Sarah Smith who lived in Church Street, Nuneaton. She became the wife of John Townsend (1813-1890). Sarah died in 1907 and was buried at Attleborough churchyard. She was pictured here outside her cottage in Attleborough. In 1841, the Townsends, then in their twenties, were living on the Turnpike Road in Attleborough, now Lutterworth Road. They moved to the Green and were later living in Bull Street. John was a grocer, and beer retailer. He probably ran one of the beer houses around Attleborough Square. Sarah was a dressmaker and passed her skills onto the children of Alfred Green, her daughter's husband. (Anne Lawson Collection)

Sarah Townsend 22 July 1887

Opposite: A beautiful Leonard Chettle photographic portrait of local girl Mary Whittaker. Leonard Chettle's studio stood nearly opposite the Co-op Hall in Queens Road between Edward Street and Norman Avenue, Leonard Chettle (1884-1963) living in the latter. He was a native of Rushden, Northamptonshire before he came to Nuneaton in 1910 when he joined the photographic firm owned by Clare Speight. In the First World War, he joined the Royal Flying Corps. He married the daughter of John Cox, a Chilvers Coton, Ribbon Weaver. He retired in 1950 when his photographic business was taken over by E.V. Openshaw. (Anne Lawson Collection)

Overleaf: King Edward VI grammar school rugby team in the 1926/27 season. John Paling (1910-1979) is the third player from back, with Rex Jeffcote to his right. John Paling was the grandson of Thomas Paling (1839-1925), the stationmaster at Nuneaton Abbey Street station for about thirty years. Rex, I believe, died young of heart disease. (Anne Lawson Collection)

Top: The Greens of Attleborough entertaining the wounded soldiers making a full recovery from their injuries at the tennis court behind their premises at the Square, Attleborough, during the First World War. (Anne Lawson Collection)

Above: Nuneaton High School Girls in the 1930s. Does anyone recognise their grandma? (Madge Edmands Collection)

Opposite: A photograph of two Nuneaton children taken at The Helios Studio, Coton Road, by F.H. Stanley, *c.* 1900. Mr Stanley took over from Marie Weale. (Dennis Labram Collection)

Above: This view was almost certainly taken for the 1907 Borough of Nuneaton celebration and shows Mr William Litchfield's float. The float has a hearth on it, and a tethered horse. It was covered with a bower of greenery over a fancy ironwork framework. The blacksmith is complete with hammer and all his tools of the trade. This smithy was later taken over by Cracknells. The smithy is still there in Bond Street if you know where to look. (Author's Collection)

Opposite below: A wedding party believed to have taken place in the spacious leafy park of Attleborough Hall next to the church where the ceremony would have been. This wedding united the Carter and Smith families. They are respectively the bride and groom in the centre of the photograph; Elizabeth Carter married John Smith around 1908. Unfortunately Jack Smith was killed during the First World War and his body was never found. They had three children, Reginald, Hubert and Norman (who died aged four). After the war, Lizzie Smith went to live at Yoxall in Derbyshire. She never remarried. Seated by the bride is the matriarch of the Carter family, Mary Jane (née Wright, *c.* 1859-1938). She was by now a widow, her husband John having died in 1907 from Bright's Disease, aged forty-nine. John was apprenticed in 1872 to the carpenter and joiner, Thomas Chaplain of Attleborough. The couple were living in William Street, Attleborough when he died. All of John's sons followed their father into the building trade. Percy Carter, a carpenter (1885-1969), is seen sitting in the middle row next to two ladies with his wife, Annie Elizabeth (née Daffern, 1884-1973) to his left. William Henry (Harry) was a painter and decorator. He is seated on the ground second from the left. Also seen is either Thomas or Frederick, seated in the centre (Tom was a bricklayer, Fred was a plumber). The two bridesmaids seated on the ground are their sisters, on the left Alice Mary (?-1959) and on the right Emma Rowley Carter (?-1961). Neither of the girls married. Their boyfriends were killed in the First World War and they never recovered from the loss. Instead they went to look after their mother until she died in 1938. The young child in the front row seated below the bride was Frederick Carter (1906-1969), the eldest son, and then only child of Percy and Annie Elizabeth. Fred had a very bad car accident in the 1960s and did not recover from the injuries he sustained. (Author's Collection)

Right: In 2003 a great friend and favourite of many Nuneatonians, Maurice Billington (b. 1930) died. A lifelong railway enthusiast, Maurice was a well-known local character. His knowledge of railways, particularly small independent companies, was encyclopaedic. His interests included cycling, singing (he was a chorister at Nuneaton church for many years) and jazz music. Not only was Maurice a good companion and true friend, he was a practising Christian who showed enormous selfless kindness to many people in times of trouble and illness. He will be sadly missed. He is pictured here in his younger days in the 1950s. In the background is Attleborough Road. (Author's Collection)

WILLS's GOLD FLAKE CIGARETTES

F C PEARCE
HAIR CUTTING & SHAVING
SALOON

'WESTWARD HO' SMOKING MIXTURE   'WESTWARD HO' SMOKING MIXTURE

FAULKNERS   FAULKNERS
NOSEGAY NOSEGAY
SHAG.   SHAG.

Frederick Charles Pearce was a native of Newbury in Berkshire and he went to Hairdressing College in Birmingham before setting up his two-seat hairdressing shop in a little wooden lean-to shop next to the Liberal Club in Abbey Street. Charlie Pearce took up chain smoking to hide the smell of all the filthy heads he had to contend with on a daily basis. If people's hair was too filthy and lice-ridden he would send them down to the slipper baths in Mill Walk to have a bath before he would deal with them. At the end of the day he would bag all the hair clippings up and send it to the lime plasters to use in their plaster on the walls of the new houses then being built in Nuneaton. So if you live in the older houses in Attleborough, Chilvers Coton, Stockingford and Nuneaton and you break into the lime plaster on the walls and see hair sticking out - think about the old townsfolk whose hair this might be. Politically correct tobacco advertising was not an important issue in Charlie's day. (Charles Pearce Collection)

Right above and below: Local historians must not ignore newspaper reports. There were three important newspapers in Nuneaton: the *Nuneaton Chronicle* (1868-1956), the *Nuneaton Observer* (1877-1980), and the *Midlands Daily Tribune* (later the *Evening Tribune*) (1895-1961). These were founded in the particular political interests of their proprietors, sponsors and readership. The *Chronicle* was founded in the Tory tradition, the *Observer* in the Liberal tradition, and the *Tribune* was a Socialist paper. The founder of the *Nuneaton Chronicle*, Frederick Duncan Robertson (1846-1916), is said to have spent a 'lifetime at work'. When Mr Robertson started the *Chronicle* in 1868 there was no newspaper printed or published in Nuneaton. Anybody who took a newspaper had to rely on the Coventry (or in a few cases the Birmingham press). The Coventry newspapers varied considerably in the amount of local information they had on the town and surrounding parishes. On balance the *Coventry Herald* had more coverage than the others. So it was a revelation when Nuneaton's first newspaper entered people's lives. What you have to remember is that few people in the labouring classes could read or write so the *Chronicle* was a big gamble. Nevertheless Mr Robertson was well advised by his father who was a railwayman. His father understood the significance of the new railway junctions in close proximity to coalfields and brickyards and the effect they would have on the town. He must have said that Nuneaton will become, in time, a boomtown, and it has. (Geoff Edmands Collection)

'Phone : 38 Nuneaton.

THE
"Nuneaton Chronicle
AND
Midland Farmers' Gazette."
Fifty-fifth year of Continuous Publication.

Telegrams : 'Chronicle,' Nuneaton.

The Recognised Organ for Auctioneers, Agriculturists, Municipal and Parliamentary Notices.

Many Years Older than any Competing Journal,

Reaches a Population of Nearly a Quarter of a Million.

Big Agricultural District.

Important Railway Centre.

Great Variety of Industries.

INCLUDING :

Engineering,

Coal-mining, Stone-quarrying, Weaving (Silks, Velvets, Plushes, Ribbons, Elastics &c,) Hatting, Hosiery, Underwear, Cottons, Wools, Box-making, Clothing, Boots and Shoes. . .

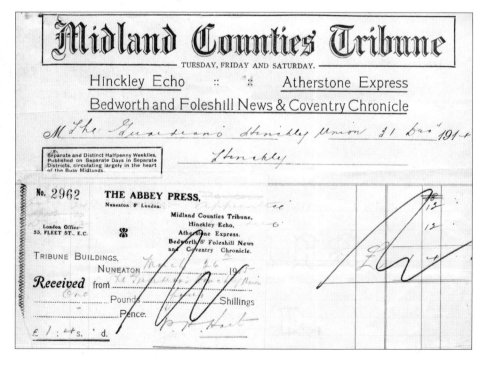

Above and below: The *Nuneaton Observer* was started by two men. One was the financial partner, the other a brilliant journalist: William Wilson (1840-1917) and Alfred Lester Scrivener (1845-1886). Alfred Scrivener's grandfather was Joseph Scrivener (1793-1859) who founded the Ropewalk in Queens Road. Alfred's father, also Joseph (1816-1860) was, at one time the Relieving Officer for the Nuneaton Union and Inspector of Nuisances. Joseph Scrivener junior accompanied the Board of Health Inspector on his tour of inspection of Nuneaton in 1849. His intimate knowledge of the town then passed to his son Alfred to whom everyone who has an interest in the history of Nuneaton must be indebted. In the first five or six years of the *Observer's* life, Alfred's interest and passion for the historic element of town life shines through. (Author's Collection)

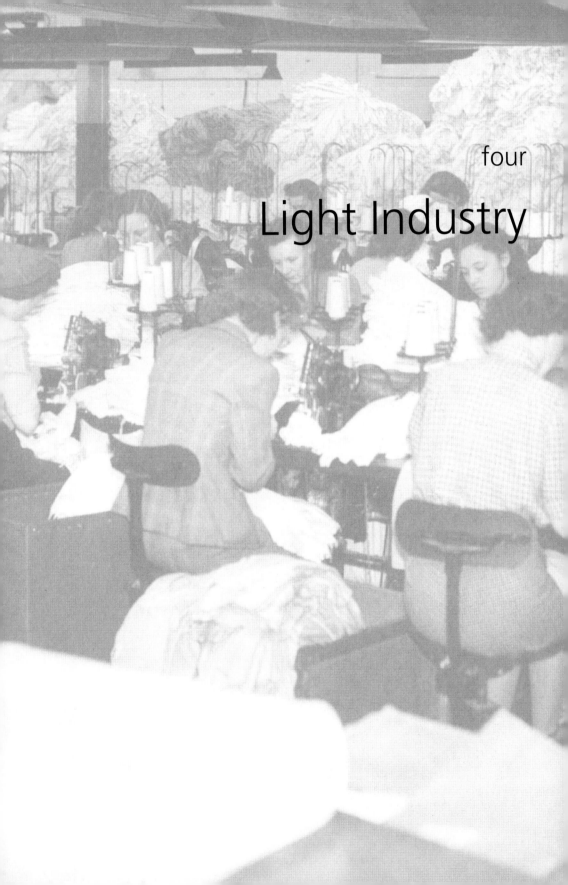

four

Light Industry

A good many attractive ladies worked at Hart & Levy's, the clothing manufacturers. This photograph may have been taken in 1907 when the town celebrated its Borough status. (Charles Mallabone Collection)

Opposite above: A later 1920s view. (Charles Mallabone Collection)

Opposite below: Is this Wood's hosiery works in Avenue Road? (Author's Collection)

Above: Anker Mills on Attleborough Road was originally built in 1858 as a cotton factory to help relieve the unemployment in the town created by the demise of the silk ribbon trade. The people that ran it came from the cotton areas of Lancashire so we see a few Lancashire families come into the area at this time and settle down around Attleborough. Unfortunately, the cotton manufacturing process was not suited to these inland climes. The cotton factory went into liquidation. It was later taken over by Fielding & Johnsons, a Leicester firm, not to be mixed up with Joseph Fielding Johnson, the Charter mayor and owner of the Union Wool & Leather Co. Fielding & Johnsons was an old established business going back to 1720. Anker Mills was acquired in 1886 under the direction of Thomas Fielding Johnson (1828-1921) who was Joseph Fielding Johnson's brother. The plant was very modern as you can see from these pictures. (Courtesy Keith Draper)

Carding on 'Platt's Card'.

Composite view of the 'New Bradford' system of worsted drawing and spinning installed in the 1950s.

Opposite below: Fielding Johnsons had two magnificent 1860 vintage Gimson steam engines, named Annie & Elizabeth, to drive the machinery. Coal was delivered by railway truck into a short siding referred to by railway men as the 'Cotton Hole Siding'. After steam generation was dispensed with at the mill, the siding went out of use and used for stabling empty coal wagons.

The end product; banding and packing 1oz. balls of hand knitting wool in attractive packaging which were sold to the wholesale trade.

Inside the works office at the Anker Mills in the 1920s. Mr James H. Padgett (centre), who lived at 16 Attleborough Road, is seen here with his assistant manager, Mr Shilton. (R.P.Neath Collection)

five

Transport and
Travel

Above: THA81 on the N43 route pulls into the Nuneaton bus station in the early '60s. (Author's Collection)

Opposite above: The major local bus company in Nuneaton was the Midland Red. It was always a pleasure to see the unique buses turned out by the Birmingham company, to listen to their distinctive engine growl and admire their cherry red livery. Tours from Nuneaton often featured these lovely thirty-seater coach type C.1s. No.3324 is seen here at Belvoir Castle on a trip from Nuneaton. The bus is in pristine condition here on 23 May 1957. (Geoff Edmands)

Opposite below: The N52 pulls out of Newdigate Street into Bondgate one wet day in September 1968. LHA263 is the bus featured here. (courtesy Keith Draper)

Inside Nuneaton Bus Garage in the early 1950s. HHA641 was type S6 No. 3040. The half cab beyond it was type SON No. 1904. (Alan Cook Collection)

Opposite: The N37 ran to Stockingford Station via Heath End Road. This unidentified SON vehicle is parked at the terminus, waiting to load up for another journey. (Alan Cook Collection)

Above and below: One of the least-known facts about Nuneaton is that it had an important aerodrome, perhaps second in importance at one time to Hendon, the London airport. Almost halfway between London and Manchester, Nuneaton was a useful stopover point for the early flyers who used to navigate by flying up the London & North Western Railway Line to Manchester. Attleborough Fields Farm just south of Nuneaton had a large flat field, ideal for these planes to set down on, refuel and be on their way again. For a short time, Attleborough Fields Aerodrome flourished with private flyers, commercial airlines and flying galas. Even the very first 'Laker Airlines' started from Nuneaton. Trevor Laker, a former motorcyclist who relished taking his life into his own hands, started a regular air service from Nuneaton in 1919. By the late 1920s the airfield was out of use and returned to agriculture. These views show some of the range of aircraft there in the immediate years after the First World War. A large wooden hanger erected by Mr E.F. Melly in 1915 was dismantled and re-erected in Riversley Park as a petrol and oil store. This was later taken down and the Riversley Park Clinic stands in its place. (Keith Draper's Collection)

Above: In the 1930s and '40s you would have seen this distinctive van around town delivering groceries to all the many little shops that stood on street corners before the advent of the supermarket.

Below: Three Austin Cambridge taxis belonging to Mr Court of Camp Hill, seen here on 12 March 1964.

A brand new fire engine for Nuneaton, built by John Morris & Sons Ltd., Salford Fire Engine Works, Manchester. (Keith Draper's Collection)

Until the early 1900s, road transport was almost the universal domain of the horse. One large horse could convey quite a large load as in this case of two enormous logs. Here, he has stopped outside Matthews, the Butchers house in Queens Road, which stood where the Kwik Save car park now is, adjacent to the Co-op Hall. The logs were probably destined for the Nuneaton Timber Company. The year is said to be 1926 and the timber had been donated by Sir F.A. Newdigate for the hearths of striking miners and their families. (Fred Phillips Collection)

six

Religious Life

The old Congregational church in Coton Road, built in 1719. (Author's Collection)

The new Congregational church of 1904 still stands. A magnificent building, it's one of the few fine Edwardian buildings to grace our townscape. (Author's Collection)

Chapel End, Nuneaton, was so called after the Chapel that was erected here. (Author's Collection)

The new oak pulpit and choir screen in Attleborough Baptist Chapel on 22 September 1963. (Author's Collection)

A musical occasion inside one of our local churches.

Opposite above: Inside the Abbey church in Manor Court Road. This photograph shows the broken masonry, which was reused in the nineteenth-century reconstruction. (Author's Collection)

Opposite below: St. Nicholas parish church and Vicarage was a pleasant corner of the old town. A gardener is rolling the lawn in front of the extensive Vicarage gardens.

ST.NICHOLAS CHURCH NUNEATON.

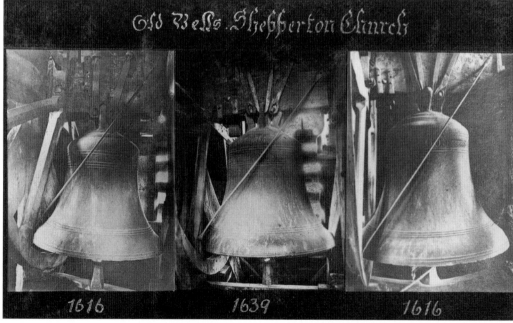

Old Bells. Shepperton Church

1616   1639   1616

CHILVERS COTON

These new bells now provide harmony for the church's bellringers. (Author's Collection)

Opposite above: Our old church dominated the approach to the town then as it does now. High wrought decorative iron railings surrounded many tombs. The churchyard was often left to become a wild field of long grass and meadow flowers. This photograph records a moment just after the long grass was cut down in an attempt to tidy up the otherwise desolate graveyard. (Author's Collection)

Opposite below: The old bells at Chilvers Coton church were known as 'Coton's discordant bells'. Because one was cracked, they were recast at Taylor's Bell foundry, Loughborough, in 1907. The oldest bells were originally cast in 1616, the year of William Shakespeare's death. (Author's Collection)

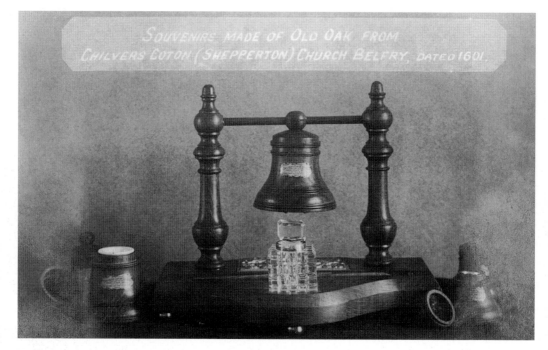

Parts from the old bells were recast into small handbells that were given to the church's bellringers. The original timber oak bell frames were made into various souvenirs including this inkstand. Old timber hewn in 1601 for the Coton bell frame was fashioned into this fine oak table, which may not have survived the bombing of 1941. (Author's Collection)

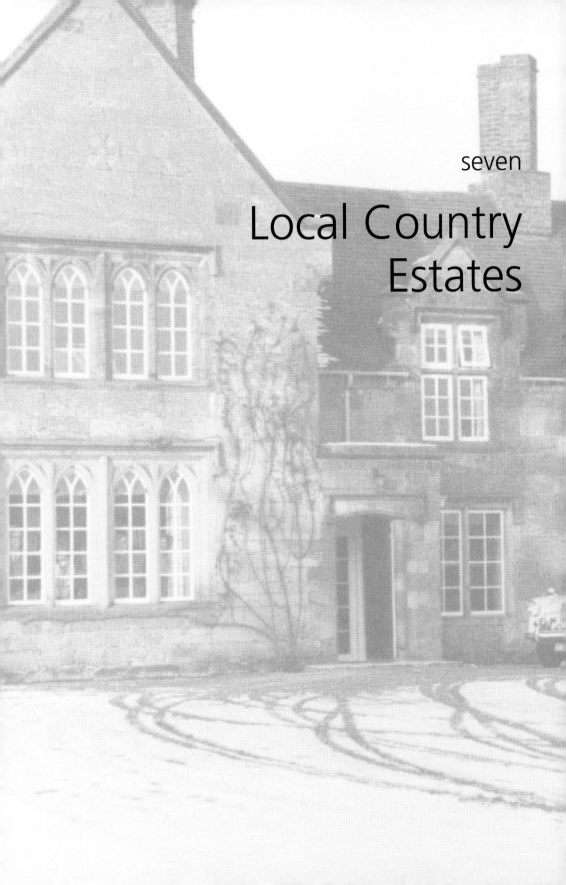

seven

Local Country Estates

This view of Church Road, Stockingford, through the gates of the estate North Lodge at the entrance to the Arbury estate was taken on 28 October 1951. It is popularly known to Nuneatonian's as 'The Round Towers'. Just visible through the gate is the tower of Stockingford church, built in 1824. It was a 'Chapel of Ease' for the people of Stockingford on Nuneaton (or Stockingford) Common. This church was immortalised as Paddiford church in *Scenes of Clerical-Janet's Repentance*, three stories written by George Eliot, which featured life in the parishes of Chilvers Coton, Astley and Nuneaton. (Geoff Edmand's Collection)

Opposite above: Temple House on the Arbury Estate, was the home of Capt. F.H.M. Fitzroy Newdegate when this photograph was taken on 27 December 1968. (Geoff Edmands)

Opposite below: Astely Castle and church, *c.* 1959.

ASTLEY CASTLE AND CHURCH (KNEBLEY), NUNEATON   L 62

Griff Lodge, Arbury, Nuneaton through which Caterina, 'that little black eyed monkey' first came to Cheveril manor in Mr Gilfil's Love Story, *Scenes of Clerical Life*, George Eliot, 1857. The canal system on the Arbury estate was an early and unique transport system of great historic importance. It is almost an ancient monument. It was built to enable mined coal on the Arbury estate to be transported to Coventry, Banbury and eventually to London. (Author's Collection)

ATTLEBOROUGH HALL. NR. NUNEATON.

Attleborough Hall was one of several country estates surrounding and hemming in the town. It stood in its own pleasure grounds which stretched from where Park Street is now, to Bull Street, Attleborough and back from Attleborough Road to the Trent Valley Railway line. These extensive grounds were laid out with fine specimen trees and shrubs, which have sadly now all gone. Covered with houses, Highfield Road cuts through, and the church was built on part of the grounds in 1842. (Author's Collection)

eight

Local Pubs

What better than a refreshing pint in a local pub? Three Nuneaton friends are home on leave or demob.

'There is no private house in which people can enjoy themselves so well as at a capital tavern. You are sure you are welcome, and the more good things you call for, the welcomer you are. There is nothing which has yet been contrived by man by which so much happiness is produced as by a good tavern or inn.' (Dr Johnson, 1776, from *Boswell's Life!*)

Nuneaton had a wide selection of old licensed premises. Pubs are important in social history because they were, and still are, the workingman's front parlour. Here they can meet with their friends with an endless supply of liquid refreshment. A whole chapter of people's lives were acted out in the bar. They were a resort of comfort in times of relaxation, in distress and in marital infidelity. Political groups, sporting clubs, friendly societies, and pub entertainments from darts and dominoes to skittles met there. Pubs were the place to chase the opposite sex, pose in your best attire, get rid of the stresses and strains of working life, and were a place of retreat from a nagging wife or a plethora of kids. Here, you could indulge in lotteries, betting, and other gaming pursuits, not to mention enjoying the warmth and clean facilities that one sometimes would not have at home. But like actors, once their part at the bar was played out, the soap opera of their lives was forgotten.

Public houses also played a key part in the commercial life of our town. The inns and hotels provided bed, board and dinner for visitors and commercial travellers, fed and watered the horses, and provided a stopping place for stage coaches. Business was contracted in the bar in the days before offices were used. Even today some of the best business deals are done over a 'pie and a pint'.

Taverns and public houses provided entertainment for the general population. They were also used as a place of business and a stopping place for carters and traders. Beer houses were found throughout the district, and were informally set up in people's front rooms where a chance of a bit of additional income could be obtained. In a town of courts and yards like Nuneaton, the owner of the plot of land with his good front house fronting the main street, who had filled up his back yard with court tenements could turn his parlour into a beer house thus scraping a few more coppers out of his hapless tenants. In October 1830 a new act of parliament removed 2s 8d beer duty from a barrel of beer and the need to be licensed on the proviso that you only sold beer. New beer houses sprung up all over the district. Many lasted as long as the proprietor could be bothered to carry on the business, and some old beer houses established back in 1830 are still going today as fully-fledged pubs, having obtained licenses to sell wines, spirits and tobacco.

The New Ropewalk shopping development will take its name from the former occupation of the proprietor of this public house, the George & Dragon, Queens Road. Joseph Scrivener (1793-1859) came to Nuneaton in about 1816. He purchased these premises and laid out an extensive ropewalk at the rear. He had ten tenement cottages built at the back of the pub known as 'Scrivener's Yard'. He also carried out ribbon weaving in the top storey of the building, and had a grocer's shop on the ground floor. To the left is Warrens, confectioner, and to the right P.&D. Stores, formerly Phillimores. This block of buildings stands ready for demolition in 1965. (Keith Draper collection)

The former Wellington (now renamed The Pig & Whistle) traces its ancestral history back to the Old Ram, Market Place. The original Ram must have been almost as old as the granting of the market charter, as Richard Jely, tenant of John Broke of London, was at 'Le Ramme' in a survey of Nuneaton dated 1543/44. Daniel Green and Thomas Bills were publicans there in the first half of the nineteenth century. In Dan Green's time it was a resort for cock-fighting. When the pub closed in the 1860s, its place was taken by the New Ram in Abbey Street (later renamed the Wellington). William Clarke was the publican at the New Ram in 1863. (Author's Collection)

The Wharf Inn of Coventry Road was built as a canal pub with warehouses for boat traffic. It was originally owned by the Arbury Estate and then was taken over by Salt's Brewery of Burton upon Trent, which was absorbed into the Bass empire. (Author's Collection)

The Virgins Inn stood here on the corner of College Street at Hill Top. It is said there was a shrine to the Virgin Mary on the corner of Coventry Road and College Street (although it only became known as College Street in the mid-nineteenth century). That is how the pub got its name; it was located at an ancient road junction known as 'Virgin's End'. (Author's Collection)

A group of Mallabones and their relatives and friends on the lawn of The Jolly Colliers posed in their Sunday best. The event is not known but the date is 25 August 1915. The patriarch of the family, Tom Mallabone, is seated in the second row from the front, second from the right. Tom and his wife had fifteen children, but only eight survived. From left to right, back row: Ann Brooks, Eliza Harris, Mary Ann Wiln (one of Tom's daughters), Wally Boon (who was killed in the First World War), Hannah and Jack Trimm (husband and wife), the next three ladies are unidentified, then Ann Hall stands at the end. Seated are Billy Wiln, Daisy Boon (Tom's daughter, who first married Wally Boon then after he was killed, married Harry Burchnall), Tommy Skeets, Lily Skeets (another of Tom's daughters), Tom Mallabone and Florrie Harris.

On the grass are Lucy Skeets *née* Mallabone with baby Eric Mallabone. We do not have the name of the other child, presumably another one of Tom's grandchildren. (Charles Mallabone Collection)

The Jolly Colliers. (Geoff Edmands)

A view along Abbey Street with Abbey Gate on the right, and Matthias Baker's Chemist Shop, and Higgs & Sons boot and shoe stores on the left. The next shop along is F.R. Jones, printer, stationer, and publisher of hundreds of collectable picture postcards. The most interesting detail of this photograph is a rare view of the Pheasant Inn (closed in 1934) with its conspicuous sign board. Its license was transferred to the Weddington Grove. (Author's Collection)

A watercolour painting of the old Grazier's Arms as it was first built, probably during the 1860s. On the left is Weddington Terrace. The roadway was then known as Derby Lane; it led, eventually, to the town of that name some forty miles away. (Percy Roe Collection)

nine

Fondly
Remembered

It is hard to imagine that this schoolroom, which was the place of education for arguably one of the greatest Victorian female novelists, survived until 1960, only to be pulled down by the council for road-widening. Mary Ann Evans (1819-1880), who used the pseudonym George Eliot when writing, was educated here between 1828 and 1832. She left to go to school in Coventry as her father wanted her to learn languages and the only school that could offer them was in the neighbouring city. It was very unusual in those days for parents to be prepared to give their female offspring such a well-rounded education. Her father was not to know this, but his far-sightedness produced one of the best writers of the nineteenth century; we owe a great debt of gratitude to Robert Evans (1773-1849). He did not live to see the success of his daughter's literary career, however, as it started eight years after his demise. (Author's Collection)

The interior of George Eliot's schoolroom. (Author's Collection)

Second Round of the Midland Senior Cup.
NUNEATON v. COVENTRY.

Players and Spectators at last Saturday's match on the Nuneaton Rugby Football Ground, Attleboro'. Nuneaton won a very good game by 4 pts. to nil.

Some scenes from a Nuneaton and Coventry Midland Senior Cup rugby match at the Harry Cleaver Ground, Attleborough, in March 1925. Nuneaton won by four points to nil. (Courtesy of Rod Grubb)

King Edward Grammar School 1898. The future great and good young men of Nuneaton are featured with well-known local names. From left to right, back row: R. Iliffe, ? Davey, ? Stewart, ? Abel, H. York, ? Knox, F.W. Wright, R. Drig, ? Blair, F. Whitehouse, ? Davey, H.N. Lilley, ? Knox, A. Clay, S. Currin, ? Paulson, L. Satchwell. Second row: A. Cox, -?-, ? Knox, A. Marriott, G. Williamson, ? Winfield, -?-, ? Wilson, ? Woodward, -?-, F. Reader, ? Porter, ? Smith, ? Paulson, ? Mayo, J. Stone, A. Roberts, W.C. Kaye, Third row: C. Sturgess, -?-, ? Lewis, A.B. Holman, Rev. S.G. Waters, Mr Butler, Mr Lowder, W.E. Lester, N. Deed, ? Dewes, -?-, ? Abel, J. Shaw, Front row: E. Clay, A.W.R. Moreton, H. Mills, K. Waters, ? Nason, ? Hughes, A. Nixon, ? Blofield, ? Stewart, ? Juby, ? Gee, J.W. French, ? Paulson. (Author's Collection)

Opposite above: There used to be a sales kiosk and tearooms in Riversley Park. The occasion is VE Day 1945 with crowds of Nuneaton folk celebrating the end of hostilities in a long forgotten part of Riversley Park. (Author's Collection)

Opposite below: Do you remember the bitter cold winters we suffered in the 1950s? This view of Sunday 30 March 1952 shows the bandstand in Riversley Park in a bleak and desolate landscape.

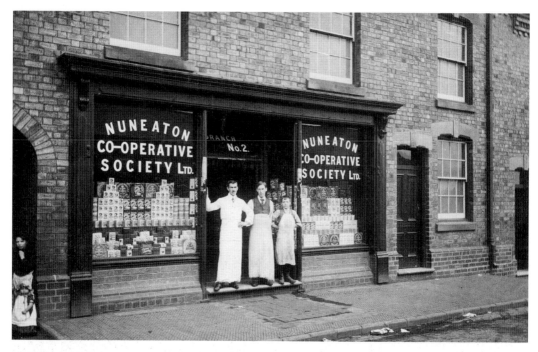

Nuneaton Co-operative Society's no.2 store, Ansley Common. The contents of the window would be collector's items today. (Author's Collection)

A selection of contemporary furniture in Nuneaton's S.&U. Stores on 25 March 1959. (Geoff Edmands)

Opposite: A parade in Abbey Street in the 1920s, although we do not know the occasion. Worthington's Cash Stores is on the left. On the far left the corner of the Pheasant Inn can be seen. The tall building above the banner is Nuneaton Liberal Club. (Author's Collection)

Nuneaton Amateurs must have produced Gilbert & Sullivan's operetta, *Mikado*, many times. This was the cast of the 1920s. (Author's Collection)

Opposite above: Another unrecorded occasion from around 1900 with Britannia in the centre. A bevy of ladies are wearing a wide variety of costumes. Could it have been to commemorate the Coronation of Edward VII? (Anne Lawson Collection)

Opposite below: The Queen's Silver Jubilee street celebrations on 7 June 1977 in Hamlet Close, Whitestone. (Geoff Edmands)

Members of Nuneaton Tennis Club pose for their photograph in 1930. (Anne Lawson Collection)

Opposite above: Prominent members of the local tennis fraternity used a court at the back of the Square in Attleborough village. Here members of the Green family pose for their photograph whilst entertaining disabled soldiers during the First Word War. (Anne Lawson collection)

Opposite below: Humphrey Millward, Technical Manager at Sterling Metals, *c.* 1950

The offices of Sterling Metals Ltd in Marston Lane, Attleborough, in the 1950s.

Opposite above and below: Two views of the interior of Sterling Metals foundry in the 1950s.

LAWYER DEMPSTER'S HOUSE, MILVERTON

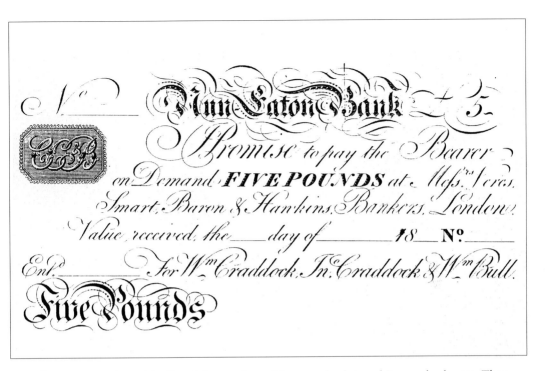

Do you remember white fivers? At one time a Nuneaton bank issued its own banknotes. They were printed by Craddock & Bulls, the local bankers. (Author's Collection)

Opposite above: Around the year 1910, if you came into Nuneaton town from Attleborough you would see that the old town was separated from the outskirts by this avenue of trees. On the right, the wall surrounding the churchyard is still there but the buildings beyond have long since gone. Beyond, the old buildings in Church Street, which were badly damaged by the air raid of May 1941, are subsequently being pulled down. (Author's Collection)

Opposite below: 'Lawyer Dempster's House' was badly damaged in the blitz of May 1941. George Eliot described it in *Janet's Repentance* as 'An old fashioned house... outside it had a rough face of stucco, and casement windows with green frames and shutters; inside it was full of long passages and rooms with low ceilings'. (Author's Collection)

Above and left: The George Eliot Fellowship was founded on 9 November 1930 by Mr A.F. Cross. Mr Cross was the Editor of the *Nuneaton Chronicle*. The first George Eliot supper was held on 22 November 1930 at the Newdigate Arms Hotel. Miss Elizabeth Haldane was the first president. The Fellowship was started to mark the fiftieth anniversary of the death of George Eliot and continues to flourish today, serving the interests of our homegrown author's international following. In many ways, George Eliot has become the First Lady of Victorian literature. She lived locally in the hamlet of Griff for the first twenty-two years of her life (1819–1841). The photograph above was taken of the second George Eliot supper on 23 November 1931. The distinguished bespectacled gentleman standing with winged collar in the centre of the picture is Dr Edward Noel Nason who had known George Eliot's family well. He said that his parents had been invited to dine with George Eliot at Griff House in December 1880 just as the authoress had developed her final fatal illness. The dinner was unfortunately cancelled. (Author's Collection)

"Surely it is not true blessedness to be free from sorrow while there is sorrow and sin in the world: Sorrow is then a part of love, and love does not seek to throw it off."

From Adam Bede

J. S. Haldane

Above: 'Surely it is not time blessedness to be free from sorrow while there is sorrow and sin in the world: sorrow is then a part of love, and love does not seek to throw it off.' (A quotation from *Adam Bede*, in the handwriting of Miss Haldane.)

Right: Mr George Lewis, one of the founder members of the George Eliot Fellowship. (Author's Collection)

2nd Anniversary Dinner 23-11-31.

Several fine houses were built in and around the town centre during the late Victorian and Edwardian period using local Stanley Brothers or Haunchwood Brick & Tile terracotta products. This is a good example in Manor Court Road. (Author's Collection)

Opposite above: The signatures of all those local worthies who attended the first George Eliot Fellowship supper.

Opposite below: George's bakery, which stood on the corner of Corporation Street and Newtown Road. Just visible at the rear is the roof of the Ritz cinema. Behind the trees to the right is the rear premises of the Coach & Horses pub. (Author's collection)

Sandwiched between the Hippodrome Theatre and Joseph Ellis's warehouse were these two old cottages. Wales's fish and chip restaurant now occupies this site. The photograph was taken in the 1950s. (Arthur Tooby)

The original intention was to start construction of Courtaulds factory in Marlborough Road just prior to the start of the First World War. Building materials were delivered but setting out had hardly taken place when war broke out, and construction was stopped. Local architect, Harry Quick (1858-1935) was the designer. In 1912, his architectural practice was at 12 Market Place. He also practised in the city of Coventry for forty-five years and was responsible for the Courtaulds factories there. All Courtaulds warm pink engineering bricks came from Webster Hemmings' brickyard in Foleshill. Gillett & Johnson of Croydon, Surrey, made its famous clock in 1920 at a cost of £1,078. Nuneaton's much-loved timepiece kept local time for seventy-four years. In 1989 the mill was sold for conversion into flats. Local clock enthusiast and conservationist, Harold Lapworth, took over the maintenance of the clock. In 1989, J.B. Joyce & Co. Ltd of Whitchurch in Shropshire, repaired the four dials. It was optimistically hoped the clock would be a feature of the Nuneaton landscape for many years. Sadly, this did not turn out to be the case. Late in 1994, in response to the deteriorating condition of the building, Beazer Homes increased its security. Consequently, Harold Lapworth was prevented from winding the clock mechanism. Local conservationists, fearing the imminent demolition of the mill, made moves to have it listed. The owners thwarted their attempts. A flurry of correspondence with the council came to nothing and the mill was unceremoniously demolished in 1995. Although the clock mechanism was saved, its future is still uncertain and it will never keep time for the people of Nuneaton again. (Author's Collection)

The fine Courtaulds canteen building in Marlborough Road survives! It has now been converted into industrial units. (Author's collection)

I have included this anonymous photograph in the hope that someone will recognise his or her relatives or the location. It is thought to be inside Courtaulds mill, but no definite information is available. (Steve Casey collection)

Other local titles published by Tempus

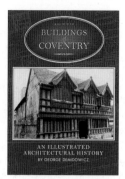

Buildings of Coventry An Illustrated Architectural History
GEORGE DEMIDOWICZ

There are one thousand statutory and locally listed buildings in the city of Coventry, and many of these are splendid examples of their period. This book describes and illustrates some of the finest examples that can be seen today and will serve as a useful guide for those wishing to explore and learn more about the city's history through its buildings. Coventry can be rightly proud of this architectural heritage.
0 7524 3115 3

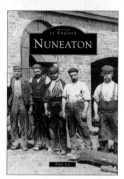

Nuneaton
PETER LEE

This earlier pictorial record of 200 photographs explores how Nuneaton has progressed and developed throughout the decades of the twentieth century. Changes that have taken place in the town can clearly be seen in images of the town centre, old shops and pubs and industries that were once important at the turn of the twentieth century, including coal mining, stone quarrying, textile production, engineering and ironfounding.
0 7524 2163 8

Stratford Canal
NICK BILLINGHAM

The Stratford Canal formed part of the inspiration for the railway network and, later, when the railways and roads appeared to threaten the annihilation of the entire canal system it was the Stratford Canal that pioneered the movement to rescue this part of our industrial heritage. Today the canal remains a fragment of the early industrial world, whilst underneath its placid waters flows a turbulent history.
0 7524 2122 0

Warwickshire County Cricket Club: 100 Greats
ROBERT BROOKE

Since Warwickshire's first and only bona fide cricket club was formed at Leamington Spa's Regent Hotel on 8 April 1882, it has enjoyed a chequered record of success and failure. There can, however, be no argument about the individual ability of the players who have represented the club over the decades. This volume offers the reader the chance to look back and recognise the achievements of the men who contributions made the county.
0 7524 2180 8

If you are interested in purchasing other books published by Tempus, or in case you have difficulty finding any Tempus books in your local bookshop, you can also place orders directly through our website

www.tempus-publishing.com

or from **BOOKPOST**, Freepost, PO Box 29, Douglas, Isle of Man, IM99 1BQ
tel 01624 836000 email bookshop@enterprise.net